Arctic Babies

Kathy Darling
Photographs by Tara Darling

Walker and Company
New York

Thank you to the New York Aquarium, a protector of Arctic wildlife, especially the orphaned walrus calves and the baby belugas they allowed us to photograph.

To the Philadelphia Zoo. For a very prickly encounter with the baby porcupine in the Children's Zoo. Thanks.

Thank you to Paul and Brenda Zimmerman, reindeer herders extraordinary, for letting us photograph the babies at Hammercreek Farm of Lititz, Pennsylvania.

To the Animal Kingdom of Bordentown, New Jersey, which has provided a home for the Arctic foxes we photographed. Thanks very much.

To Lyle Jensen of New England Alive in Ipswich, Massachusetts, who rescues wild critters in need and then sets them free. We salute you and thank you for letting us share the baby squirrels and owl.

Thank you to the VonHaggin family of Flag Acres Zoo in Hoosick Falls, New York, devoted and loving guardians of the Siberian tiger and Canadian lynx babies we had the pleasure to photograph.

To the North American Wolf Foundation for allowing us to photograph the new babies at Wolf Hollow in Ipswich, Massachusetts. Thanks.

Text copyright © 1996 by Kathy Darling
Photographs copyright © 1996 by Tara Darling

First published in the United States of America in 1996 by Walker Publishing Company, Inc.; first paperback edition published in 1997.

Published simultaneously in Canada by Thomas Allen & Son Canada, Limited, Markham, Ontario

Library of Congress Cataloging-in-Publication Data
Darling, Kathy.
Arctic babies / Kathy Darling; photographs by Tara Darling.
p. cm.
Summary: Photographs and text describe some of the young animals that are found in the frigid Arctic regions, including moose, foxes, walrus, porcupines, reindeer, and whales.
ISBN 0-8027-8413-5 (hardcover). —ISBN 0-8027-8414-3 (reinforced)
1. Zoology—Arctic regions—Juvenile literature. 2. Mammals—Arctic regions—Infancy—Juvenile literature.
3. Birds—Arctic regions—Infancy—Juvenile literature. [1. Zoology—Arctic regions. 2. Animals
—Infancy.] I. Darling, Tara. II. Title.
QL105.D36 1996
591.998—dc20   95-37736
ISBN 0-8027-7504-7 (pbk.)

Map on page 3 and arctic icons throughout the book by Dennis O'Brien.
Artwork on page 32 by Linda Howard and Elizabeth Sieferd.
Printed in Hong Kong
4 6 8 10 9 7 5 3

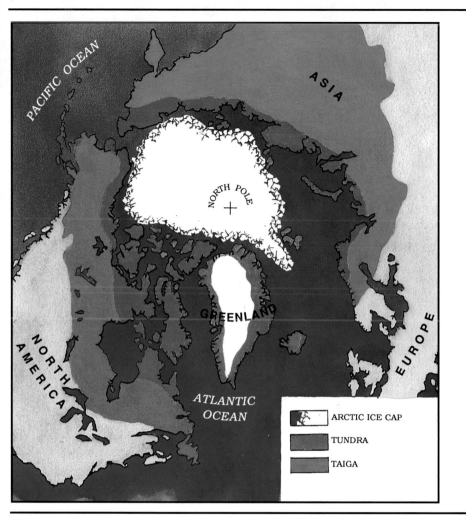

| ICE CAP | TUNDRA | TAIGA |

These symbols appear throughout the book and represent the region of the Arctic that each animal inhabits. For more information about these regions turn to "About the Arctic" on the last page of the book.

Cold. Shivery cold. Snowy cold. Icy cold. Blizzard cold. The Arctic is any kind of cold you can think of. In summer it is cold. In winter it is *very* cold. And that *very* cold, very dark winter lasts more than half the year.

Even so, there is life in the Arctic. You will be surprised to discover that the far North is a good place to find babies. These are special babies—wrapped up in packages of fur, feather, or fat to keep out the cold.

Polar bears and harp seals have birthdays on the coldest, darkest days of winter. But most of the northland babies are born in the spring or summer. That's why you don't see ice or snow in some of the pictures.

Come with us to some of the last wild places and see what's new in the North.

TAIGA

Lynx

Lynx kittens are copycats. They copy their mother. By copying everything she does, they learn survival skills. Mother lynx gives her babies almost a year of lessons, helping them through the snowy winter. Then she practices tough love and chases the kittens away to make room for new babies.

As curious as any other cat, these two-week-old lynx kittens are ready to explore the world outside their hollow log home. As they grow, their fur will become sandy brown and the baby blue of their eyes will turn to yellow. Their little feet will grow into big "snowshoe" paws so they can walk on crusty snow. And their legs will grow long so they can walk through deep snowdrifts in search of food.

Lynx
(Canadian Lynx)

* Baby name: Kitten
* Birthplace: Hollow log, den of earth or stone
* Birth weight: 7 ounces
* Adult weight and length: 40 pounds 40 inches
* Littermates: 1 or 2
* Favorite food: Babies drink milk; adults eat meat of rabbits, squirrels, birds.
* Parent care: Mother keeps kittens with her for 10 months. Father does not help.
* Enemies: Humans
* Home: Taiga of North America

TAIGA

TUNDRA

Moose

Mama moose is a kickboxer. She's seven feet tall, weighs a ton, and for one year this awesome parent protects her baby with her flying feet.

Wherever this supermom goes, the baby goes. Not always willingly. When the cow wades into a pond to eat water weeds, the calf complains about the cold water. It sobs and protests every step of the way.

In the fall when these giant deer choose new mates, a cow watches how the bulls treat her baby. If a bull moose is not nice to her 450-pound calf, she will drive the bull away. To a mama moose, the safety of her calf is the most important thing in the world.

Moose
(North American Moose)

* Baby name: Calf
* No specific birthplace prepared by parents.
* Birth weight and height: 25 pounds, 3 feet. Weighs 450 pounds at 6 months.
* Adult weight and height: Males can weigh up to 2,000 pounds but average 1,300. Antlers alone can weigh 50 pounds. Height is 7 1/2 feet tall.
* Littermates: 1 or 2
* Favorite food: Babies drink milk; adults eat plants.
* Parent care: Mother feeds and protects baby for 1 year. Father does not help.
* Enemies: Wolves, bears, humans
* Home: Taiga forests and marshy tundra throughout the Arctic

Owl

Who? Who? Who can see directly behind its head? The great horned owl, that's who. An owl doesn't have eyes in the back of its head, but it can see what's going on behind it by turning its head completely around. The owl's big yellow eyes are not movable. So the owl must move its whole head to see things around it.

The "horns" of a great horned owl aren't horns at all. They are just tufts of feathers. The owl uses them like eyebrows, showing how it is feeling. The baby on this page is making an expression that shows his curiosity.

Owl
(Great Horned Owl)

* Baby name: Chick
* Birthplace: Tree nest
* Birth weight: About the size of a newborn chicken (2 ounces)
* Adult weight and height: 5 pounds, 20 inches. Females are bigger than males.
* Littermates: 1 or 2
* Favorite food: Meat from small mammals or birds, insects
* Parent care: Both parents feed babies
* Enemies: Lynx, wolverine
* Home: Taiga forests of North America

TAIGA

Porcupine

A porcupine is born with thirty thousand quills! Ouch!

Don't worry. The mother isn't hurt. A newborn porcupine's quills are soft for the first few hours.

After that, watch out. These are babies that throw temper tantrums if they don't get their way. They growl, stamp their feet, release stink bombs, rattle their quills, and attack—backward! Swinging their tiny tails, they drive the needle-sharp quills into anything they hit. Porcupines can grow as many of these special hairs as they need. Any quills that break off are replaced in a few weeks.

Porcupine
(North American Porcupine)

* Baby name: Kit
* No specific birthplace prepared by parents.
* Birth weight: 1 3/4 pounds
* Adult weight and length: 15 to 25 pounds, 30 inches
* Littermates: None
* Favorite food: Babies drink milk for 2 or 3 weeks. Adults eat roots, berries, seeds, nuts, flowers, tree bark, and buds.
* Parent care: Mother cares for baby alone.
* Enemies: Fisher (a kind of weasel), occasionally lynx
* Home: Taiga of North America

Squirrel

There are two kinds of tree squirrels in the northern forests, but they don't meet very often.

Red squirrels, pictured below, are daytime squirrels. They spend the summer and fall building huge storage nests of seeds. In the winter, families cuddle together in a hollow tree and wrap their fluffy tails around themselves for warmth. Young red squirrels like to play games with their brothers and sisters. Favorite squirrel games are pinecone toss and hide-and-seek. The kits like to play chase and have climbing contests too.

Flying squirrels, pictured at left and above, are nighttime squirrels. Their name is a little joke. Squirrels can't really fly. They glide very well, though. Mother squirrel is the flight instructor and the leader of the family gliding games.

The newborn babies aren't old enough to begin lessons, but this six-week-old kit has already learned how to do loops and spirals.

Squirrel
(Red Squirrel and Northern Flying Squirrel)

* Baby name: Kit
* Birthplace: Leaf-lined nest in a hollow tree
* Birth weight: Flying squirrel, 1/10 ounce; red squirrel, 1/4 to 1/2 ounce
* Adult weight: Flying squirrel, 5 ounces; red squirrel, 3 pounds
* Littermates: Flying squirrel, 1 or 2; red squirrel, an average of 5 but could be as many as 10
* Favorite food: Babies drink milk; adults eat pine seeds, nuts, tree bark, and buds.
* Parent care: Babies are cared for by mother and live in a nest shared by a large family. Everybody cuddles together for warmth.
* Enemies: Flying squirrel's enemies are owls, lynx; red squirrel's are hawks, lynx, wolverine. In addition, both are prey of the pine martin, a kind of weasel.
* Home: Pine forests of the taiga throughout the Arctic

Tiger

Tigers are the only wild cat with stripes. Each animal has a different pattern. The special markings of white, black, and orange can identify one of these big cats, just as your fingerprints can identify you.

This six-week-old Siberian tiger cub, however, can actually change its stripes. Like many other animals of the Arctic, a Siberian tiger has fur that changes color with the seasons. The summer coat has reddish stripes. In winter the red stripes are replaced with pale yellow ones. Stripes are good camouflage, but even without them you would have a hard time finding one of these cats. There are fewer than two hundred Siberian tigers left in the wild.

Tiger
(Siberian Tiger)

* Baby name: Cub
* No specific birthplace prepared by parents.
* Birth weight: 3 pounds
* Adult weight: Males can weigh up to 850 pounds but average 600 pounds. Females average 400 pounds. Siberians are the biggest tigers.
* Littermates: 2 or 3
* Favorite food: Babies drink milk for 5 or 6 months. Adults eat the meat of deer, wild pig, fish.
* Parent care: Mother provides total care.
* Enemies: Humans
* Home: Taiga forests of Russia

Falcon

Meet the peregrine falcon—fastest creature on earth. This sky hunter is two times as fast as a cheetah. Faster even than a race car. The dive of a falcon has been timed at an awesome 250 miles per hour.

Both the mother and father peregrine use the high-speed dive to kill other birds for their babies to eat.

The chicks, dressed in fluffy white baby feathers, are born on a bare rocky ledge. In four months they will have grown all the strong feathers they need for flight. But the parents have to do a lot of coaxing to get the babies to jump off the cliff for the first time.

Falcon
(Peregrine Falcon)

* Baby name: Chick
* Birthplace: Prefers rocky cliff but if none available will lay eggs on open tundra.
* Birth weight: 1/2 ounce
* Adult weight and length: Average 3 pounds, 15 to 19 inches. Females are bigger than males.
* Littermates: 2 or 3
* Favorite food: Mainly birds, sometimes mice and voles.
* Parent care: Both parents bring food to babies.
* Enemies: Chicks and eggs are eaten by Arctic foxes, owls, and gulls. Adults are hunted by humans.
* Home: *Peregrine* means "wanderer." The falcons follow birds to tundra areas throughout the Arctic in the spring and leave with them in the fall.

TUNDRA | ICE CAP

 # FOX

Arctic foxes can take the cold better than almost any other animal. The white foxes don't even start to shiver till it is seventy degrees below zero (F). The fox pictured near right is an adult. In the winter adult foxes are so warm in their coats of white or silvery blue they follow polar bears onto the pack ice hoping to snatch some scraps when the great beasts are not looking.

Arctic fox kits are born in huge underground dens on the tundra. There are sometimes more than a hundred tunnels leading in and out.

Fox
(Arctic Fox)

* Baby name: Cub or kit
* Birthplace: Earth den on the tundra
* Birth weight: 2 1/2 ounces
* Adult weight: 6 to 10 pounds
* Littermates: Usually 3 to 4 but can be up to 10
* Favorite food: Babies drink milk; adults eat meat, eggs, and insects.
* Parent care: Food is brought by both parents.
* Enemies: Polar bears, humans
* Home: Tundra in summer, tundra and ice cap in winter throughout the Arctic

Reindeer

Marching. Marching. Reindeer are always marching. Baby reindeer can walk a few minutes after they are born, and an hour later they are able to keep up with the marching herd. A calf has a long way to walk in its lifetime. Reindeer, or caribou as they are called in North America, are the world's champion walkers. Their thousand-mile journey across the treeless, trackless tundra each year is the longest migration made by any land animal.

Female reindeer have antlers (other female deer do not). The caribou cow and her calf, pictured below, are

both starting to grow antlers. She will use them to clear away the snow to find food. The baby's antlers will be small, and it will stay near its mother during the winter, eating the food she uncovers.

Reindeer/Caribou
(European Reindeer/Barren-Ground Caribou)

* Baby name: Calf
* No specific birthplace prepared by parents.
* Birth weight and height: 10 to 20 pounds, about 16 inches tall
* Adult weight: Some kinds of reindeer weigh 175 pounds, and others are more than 600 pounds.
* Littermates: None
* Favorite food: Babies drink only milk. At one month they begin to eat plants. Adults eat plants, mostly grass and lichens.
* Parent care: Mother raises baby for 2 years.
* Enemies: Wolves, bears, humans
* Home: Reindeer are from Europe and Asia; caribou are from North America. Some herds live in the taiga in winter; others stay on open tundra. All live on tundra in summer.

TUNDRA TAIGA

Wolf

We call it the *gray* wolf, but it can be any color from white to black. We also call it the *timber* wolf, but the cry of the pack can be heard just about anywhere in the Arctic. This six-week-old cub (facing page) is just big enough to squeak out a few high notes when the pack begins to howl.

Because the animals they eat are wanderers, the wolves must be wanderers too. Unlike the babies of reindeer and moose, newborn wolf cubs cannot travel. So the pack must settle down near a rocky cave or earth den for a few months. It is only a temporary home. As soon as the cubs are able to travel, the pack hits the road again.

Wolf
(Gray Wolf)

* Baby name: Pup or cub
* Birthplace: Earth den or rock cave
* Birth weight and length:
  5 or 6 ounces, 6 to 8 inches
* Adult weight: 50 to 75 pounds.
  (about the size of a German Shepherd dog)
* Littermates: 3 to 6
* Favorite food: Babies drink milk; adults eat meat of rabbits, lemmings, caribou, or moose.
* Parent care: Whole pack helps care for babies.
* Enemies: Humans
* Home: Taiga and tundra throughout the Arctic. Many packs follow caribou herds.

Bear

Beware the polar bear! But not right away. The cub, which will become the largest meat eater on earth, is born without any teeth. A newborn polar bear can't see you or hear you either. The future king of the ice is so small and helpless that it can't even walk for a month. The baby's white fur is too short to keep it warm. Without their mother, baby bears would never survive. She builds a snow cave for her cubs, cuddles them in her warm fur, and feeds them rich milk.

It takes years of training for polar bears to become polar bears. Much of their behavior is learned.

Polar bear cubs take time out from their lessons to have fun. They especially like to make snowballs. The bigger the better.

Bear
(Polar Bear)

* Baby name: Cub
* Birthplace: Snow cave
* Birth weight and length:
  1 1/2 pounds, 1 foot
* Adult weight: Males usually about
  1,000 pounds but can be up to 1,800
  pounds. Females average 700 pounds.
* Littermates: 1 or 2
* Favorite food: Babies drink milk.
  Adults eat seals in winter; fish, birds,
  eggs, seaweed, and berries in summer.
* Parent care: Mother feeds babies and
  teaches them to hunt for two years.
  Father often kills babies.
* Enemies: Killer whale, walrus herds,
  ice (they get trapped and can't breathe
  or get crushed), and especially humans.
* Home: Along the edge of the ice pack
  all around the Arctic Circle

Seal

Harp seals are good mothers—but only for ten days.

Then they abandon their pups on the tumbled sea ice. In the darkest, coldest days of the Arctic winter, the pups are left to survive on their own. And, surprisingly, they do.

For a few days the babies cry for food. Then, when the starving infants realize mother is not going to come back, they crawl to the sea, slide in, and teach themselves to swim and hunt.

The newborn pup's furry coat, which is stained yellow from birth fluids for a few hours, soon becomes snowy white. When the baby is ready to leave the ice, its white camouflage jacket is replaced by a spotted gray one designed to hide the little water baby from dangers in the sea.

Seal
(Harp Seal)

* Baby name: Calf or pup
* Birthplace: Tumbled sea ice
* Birth weight and length: 20 pounds, 2 feet. 70 pounds at 10 days old.
* Adult weight and length: 400 pounds, 6 feet. Males and females about the same size.
* Littermates: None
* Favorite food: Babies drink only milk for 10 to 14 days. Then they eat shrimp, the tiny sea animals called *krill*, and small fish. Adults eat fish.
* Parent care: Mother cares for baby up to 2 weeks.
* Enemies: Polar bears, killer whales, humans, ice
* Home: Arctic seas and nearby areas of the North Atlantic

Walrus

Walrus do everything in a group. They are team players. Without the strength of their herd, walrus would not be able to protect their babies from polar bears and killer whales.

When danger threatens, adult walrus form a circle with their sharp tusks pointing toward the enemy. The babies ride piggyback on their mothers in the center.

A calf is born with whiskers and tusks, but the sharp little teeth don't begin to show beneath its lips for several years. When the tusks are about a foot long, the young walrus will be allowed to take a place in the circle and help protect younger babies.

Walrus
(Pacific Walrus)

* Baby name: Calf
* Birthplace: Unknown. Either on an ice floe or in sea. Nobody has ever seen a birth.
* Birth weight and length: 100 to 150 pounds, 4 feet
* Adult weight and length: Males, up to 4,000 pounds, 9 to 12 feet long; females, up to 2,700 pounds, 7 to 10 feet long
* Littermates: None
* Favorite food: Babies drink milk; adults eat meat in form of clams, crabs, snails, worms, and seals.
* Parent care: Mother feeds baby for 2 years. Whole herd protects babies.
* Enemies: Polar bears, killer whales, humans, ice
* Home: Arctic seas and nearby areas in both Atlantic and Pacific Oceans

ICE CAP

Whale

When a baby beluga is hungry, it calls for milk. The cry may be like the chirp of a canary, the baa of a lamb, the whinny of a horse, or the grunt of a pig. A white whale calf can make so many noises that you might think there is a barnyard under the sea!

Whale talk can be more than just talk, though. The echoing sounds help whales find their way and avoid accidents. A whale could get hurt if it bumped its head on an iceberg.

Little white whales, as you can see, aren't white. They are gray—like the Arctic Ocean. As a baby beluga grows, its color gets lighter and lighter. At five years old, the calf is as white as its parents.

Whale
(Beluga Whale)

* Baby name: Calf
* Birthplace: Arctic sea
* Birth weight and length:
  175 pounds, 5 feet
* Adult weight and length: Up to
  4,000 pounds, 12 to 15 feet
* Littermates: None
* Favorite food: Babies drink only
  milk for the first year. In the
  second year, they add clams,
  crabs, and worms. Adults eat
  fish, shrimp, octopus.
* Parent care: Mother feeds and
  protects baby for 2 years. Whales
  live in a big group called a *pod*
  or *herd*.
* Enemies: Polar bears, killer whales,
  humans, ice
* Home: Arctic seas. Near edge of
  ice cap in winter and in shallow
  water close to land in summer.

About the Arctic

People don't always agree about where the Arctic ends. But everybody agrees on where it starts—at the top of the world in a spot called the North Pole. This is the center of a land known as the Arctic.

There isn't actually any land under the North Pole. It lies in the middle of a frozen ocean.

All around that ice-covered sea are flat, treeless plains called *tundra*. They too are frozen for most of the year. You might expect the tundra to be buried under a thick layer of snow, but the tundra is a desert. Strong winds blow away the relatively little snow that falls. These winter winds are so strong they can knock a grown man to the ground and nothing grows very tall on the tundra because of it. The summer sun only melts the top few inches of dirt. Beneath that, the land never thaws.

South of the tundra are the vast evergreen forests of the *taiga*. Taiga covers a tenth of the land on earth—as much as the tropical rain forests.

All three of these places—the polar sea, the tundra, and the taiga—are Arctic places. Each has a group of plants and animals that have found ways to survive in the cold and the dark.

In the winter, the northern part of the earth tilts away from the sun and it doesn't appear in the sky for months and months. The only relief from the darkness is moonlight and the strange dancing lights of the *aurora borealis*. In the summer, the Arctic tilts toward the sun, and there is the constant daylight known as the *midnight sun*.

In winter and in summer, all living things in the Arctic fight a terrible enemy—the killer known as cold. Life survives in this frigid land, but just barely. This place pushes life to the limit. Damage to this ecosystem is difficult to repair. It is on the very edge of extinction. We must protect the last remaining Arctic wilderness so there will be Arctic babies forever.